The Igloo

The Igloo

Charlotte and David Yue

Houghton Mifflin Company   Boston

Library of Congress Cataloging-in-Publication Data

Yue, Charlotte.
  The igloo.

  Bibliography: p.
  Includes index.
  Summary: Describes how an igloo is constructed and
the role it plays in the lives of the Eskimo people.
Also discusses many other aspects of Eskimo culture
that have helped them adapt to life in the Arctic.
    1. Eskimos—Dwellings—Juvenile literature.
  2. Indians of North America—Dwellings—Juvenile
literature. 3. Igloos—Juvenile literature.
  [1. Eskimos—Dwellings. 2. Igloos. 3. Indians of
North America—Dwellings] I. Yue, David. II. Title.

E99.E7Y84   1988   920.004'97   88-6154
RNF ISBN 0-395-44613-9   PA ISBN 0-395-62986-1

Printed in the United States of America

HAL   10 9 8 7 6 5 4

To Emmalyn and Sebastian

Contents

The Igloo

The People and the Land

CHAPTER ONE

The People Who Lived in Igloos

Travelers to the Arctic have always been fascinated by the glistening mounds of snow that served as cozy winter homes for the native people. The people who made their homes near the top of the world inhabited the extreme northern edge of the land on earth where living things can survive. The problems they had to solve building shelter in the Arctic were as complex and difficult as those faced today by people designing spaceships. The Arctic is unforgiving. Anyone or anything unprepared to face its rigorous demands will perish. Trees cannot grow there. Vegetation of any kind is sparse. Few species of animals can exist in such a harsh and exacting climate.

Dwellers in the Arctic must face intense cold that

cracks and breaks all that it touches, devastating storms with freezing winds, and endless fields of snow that seem to have no horizon. Hunger is a constant threat. During part of the year, the sun never rises and a darkness settles that can drive people mad. Another part of the year, the sun never sets; days blur as the midnight sun circles the sky.

Yet by some human miracle, people have survived in this hostile region for thousands of years. These people call themselves Inuit, Inupiat, Yupik, or Kalâtdlit — words meaning "The Real People." They eventually came to be called Eskimos by the Europeans and Americans who encountered them. Eskimos succeeded in adapting to the Arctic by their ingenuity and patience and by understanding their world. It might seem that in such a severe environment with so few materials available people would not be able to produce many things, and those they produced would be of poor quality. But the Eskimos used the little they had for the most benefit. Bones, animal skins, stones, and even snow and ice took the place of wood that is so important to most people. They invented specialized tools and elaborate equipment for every task. But even when they did not have a tool with them, or when an important implement was lost or damaged, it did not keep them from doing the work they set out to do. They devised something else that could do the job.

Eskimos almost seemed able to create something out of nothing. The snow igloo, which used the surround-

2

ing snow as protection from freezing cold and wind, was one of the Eskimos' most ingenious and spectacular inventions. These snowhouses enabled the Central Eskimos of what is now Canada to survive the Arctic winter. They were able to live on the sea ice and hunt the animals that supplied them with food and fuel.

Snowhouses could not be lived in throughout the year in any region of the Arctic. Some Eskimo people never lived in snowhouses. But for many people snow was the only building material available in sufficient quantities that could provide adequate winter shelter. Skin tents were not warm enough for winter. Other materials could not be found on sea ice and were very difficult to transport. Snow has layers of trapped air. It protects plants and small animals by holding in the warmth of the earth and keeping out the cold air. Larger animals burrow into drifts of snow or allow a snow blanket to cover them. Eskimos skillfully used the insulating properties of snow in building snow igloos.

Eskimos lived by hunting. Almost all of their food and clothing and most of their tools and utensils came from animals. They learned many things by observing the sea and land animals that had adapted to the difficult conditions of the Arctic. Eskimos may even have learned to make igloos by imitating the polar bear's den.

It is hard to find out much about the origins of igloos since most of the evidence has long since melted away. But scientists have been able to piece together the history of the people who live in the Arctic using the arti-

facts and information they have gathered. And they can speculate about the story of the development of snow-houses.

The original settlers in the Arctic probably came from Asia across the Bering Strait when Russia and Alaska were joined by a land bridge. Some of the earliest people to settle in the Arctic used distinctive small tools of chipped stone to make arrow tips, harpoon heads,

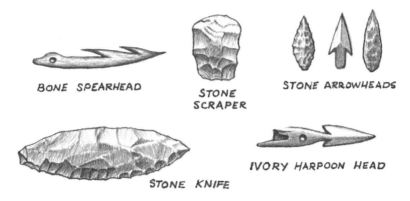

BONE SPEARHEAD

STONE SCRAPER

STONE ARROWHEADS

STONE KNIFE

IVORY HARPOON HEAD

needles, and other tools of wood, bone, and ivory. They are usually referred to as the Small Tool Culture.

These people were later followed by a group of people that anthropologists call the Norton Culture. Artifacts from this culture were discovered around the area of Norton Sound in Alaska. The Norton people came to Alaska by the same route as those of the Small Tool Culture. They must have been successful hunters. They had one-man boats called kayaks that they used for hunting on water. They used toggle-headed harpoons that could not easily slip out from wounded prey.

5

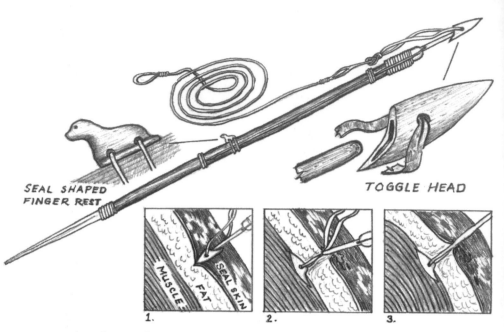

SEAL SHAPED
FINGER REST

TOGGLE HEAD

MUSCLE

FAT

SEAL SKIN

1.

2.

3.

At about the same time, a different group of people settled what is now the northern coast of Canada and eventually spread all the way to Greenland. Early discoveries of their culture were made in the Cape Dorset area, so scientists call them the Dorset peoples; some believe they were the originators of the snowhouse. They had ivory snow knives for cutting blocks of snow and soapstone lamps to heat their houses. Dorset people had kayaks like the people of the Norton culture. They also had sleds, which were probably pulled by men. With better technology their hunting range increased; they could hunt on sea ice and in open water. When hunters were on a long journey, they could take shelter from the cold in temporary dwellings made from the snow.

Later another group of immigrants made their way

to Alaska across the Bering Strait. These people have been named the Thule Culture, after a site found near the settlement of Thule in Greenland. Thule people were the ancestors of Eskimos. They were skilled whale hunters. In Alaska they constructed homes using whalebone, sod, and driftwood. During warming trends in the climate, the whales they hunted moved into the new feeding grounds that opened up as ice melted. The Thule people followed the whales eastward, moving all the way to Greenland.

The Dorset culture that had dominated Canada disappeared. In the competition for the limited resources of the Arctic, they may have been less successful than the Thule. But Thule people had learned to make snow igloos and sleds from the Dorset people, and these became essential parts of the Thule culture.

Thule people were very flexible. They adapted their hunting techniques and tools to meet changes in the climate and other conditions. They moved their settlements to follow the animals that they needed for survival. When the population of the animals that sustained them grew too small, they made changes in their diet, eating more plentiful animals. Sometimes they worked together in large groups; other times they found they could hunt more successfully if they split into small groups and scattered in search of available food.

Each culture came to view the land more appreciatively and came to understand more about the animals

that lived in the Arctic. Each culture created more specialized tools and techniques to meet their needs. People learned to make better use of the limited materials available and to build houses that responded successfully to the environment. Each group was learning to collaborate with nature rather than trying to dominate and conquer it.

When European explorers and traders ventured into

8

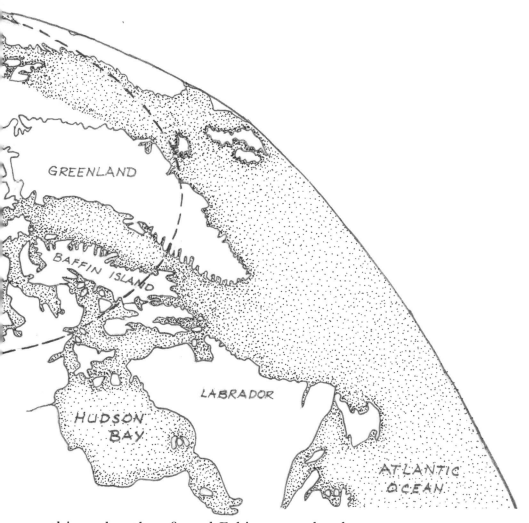

this realm, they found Eskimo people who were so successful in coping with the Arctic that their way of life extended for about six thousand miles — a greater distance than any other people in the world. People with similar customs, activities, tools, weapons, crafts, and language encircled the top of the globe from the northeast coast of Siberia in Asia, across the Arctic coast of North America, to the eastern shores of Greenland.

9

The Arctic

In the temperate zone, we are used to certain proportions of light and darkness each day. For us, the sun rises every day in the east and sets in the west. But the rhythms of the Arctic are altogether different. Even the kinds of light and the ways in which the land reflects the light are very different in the polar regions.

As the earth rotates, the surface that faces the sun is in light while the surface away from the sun lies in darkness. But because the earth is tilted, the northern and southern hemispheres receive different amounts of sunlight over the course of the year. This accounts for the seasons of the year as well as the changes in the amount of daylight throughout the year. The effects are most pronounced in the polar regions.

The total number of hours of darkness and light in one year does not really differ much from the equator to the poles, but the seasonal distribution is very different and causes completely different patterns of events in each region of the globe.

The Arctic is called the Land of the Midnight Sun. During the brief summer, the sun appears to circle round and round the sky above the horizon without ever setting. As autumn approaches, day and night become distinct again. All too soon nights grow longer and days shorter. The short days end with pale colors that fade into a black night. The sun appears less and less frequently — a few hours a day, then only for minutes. The moon, which had gone unnoticed in the days of sunlight, appears huge as it illuminates the purple sky. It seems to change its shape in the rising mists.

When the long winter sets in, it brings weeks of darkness relieved only by the milky blue of reflected moonlight, the bright stars, and the purplish twilight when the sun is not far below the horizon. Yet in the midst of complete darkness, the aurora borealis suddenly makes the world as bright as day. Ribbons of green, edged with pink and yellow, and sparkling purples and reds flicker and dance across the sky. Then the lights go out like a candle, leaving everything in darkness again. At last spring brings the good sun above the horizon again,

making orange and red patterns on the ice and blue shadows on the snow. Days grow longer once again. As another summer draws near, the sun sets so close to the horizon that there is not really darkness, just a clear yellow twilight. Soon the sun will again seem to circle the sky all twenty-four hours.

The nearer a region is to the North Pole, the longer the periods of complete darkness and of intervals when the sun never sets. But the entire area above the Arctic Circle has at least one day when the sun never sets and one day when the sun never rises.

In the polar regions, the rays of the sun strike the

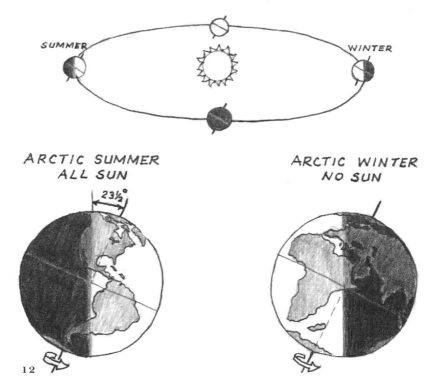

SUMMER   WINTER

ARCTIC SUMMER   ARCTIC WINTER
ALL SUN   NO SUN

23½°

earth's surface at a wide angle and spread over a large area. The rays must pass through a thick layer of insulating atmosphere before reaching the surface of the globe. When there is ice and snow on the ground, much of the heat is reflected back into the atmosphere and lost. Each ray of sun has the same intensity but the effect is weakened at higher latitudes. This is why the Arctic is so cold and why it is a land of ice and snow. Large expanses of the sea are frozen, giving the area its vast white appearance. When snow falls, most of it stays

throughout the winter since there is not enough warmth from the sun to melt it. But the total yearly precipitation is very low. The Arctic is very dry — a frozen desert. The low temperatures are combined with strong winds, causing huge drifts of snow and making exposure very hazardous for plants, animals, and people. The Arctic climate tests the survival abilities of all its inhabitants.

When the sun's warmth returns, the great fields of ice loosen. Ice floes are driven apart and crash together, sending fountains of water into the air. Breakup comes as early as June in some regions, as late as August in others. The snow melts, but the ground of the Arctic tundra a few feet below the surface is permafrost: it stays permanently frozen year round. Moisture cannot penetrate this permafrost and gets trapped in the surface layer of earth. The ground becomes spongy and difficult to walk on.

Plants that have adapted to the Arctic have short life cycles, coming to life in summer with a brief flourish. Purple, yellow, and white flowers blossom all over the hills. The warm air hums with insects and fills with the cries of the birds that have returned to their summer nesting grounds. Salmon and other fish swim and spawn in the clear streams. Even in midsummer there

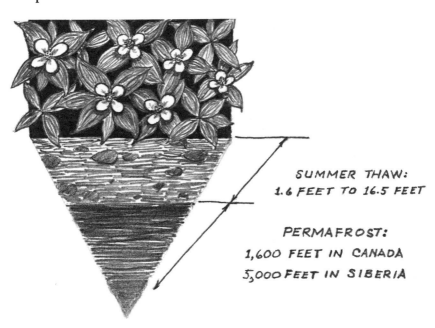

SUMMER THAW:
1.6 FEET TO 16.5 FEET

PERMAFROST:
1,600 FEET IN CANADA
5,000 FEET IN SIBERIA

KING EIDER

may be frosts and snow; no month is completely free from snow. Although air temperatures may be low, it feels warm from the radiant heat of the long hours of sunshine.

When summer ends, the colors fade. The birds fly south once more, leaving the ravens, owls, ptarmigans, and the few other kinds of birds that are permanent residents of the Arctic. The land seems gray and dismal. Lakes and rivers become covered with ice toward the end of September and ice forms around the shore. Soon there will be solid ice where the open water had been. The region is covered with snow from the beginning of October until mid-June or early July. In winter the ground rumbles with cold and cracks with frost. The world of snow and ice is monotonous and lifeless. Winter is a time of hardship. Food is scarce and hunting the few available animals is made more difficult by the darkness and the severe weather conditions. Without trees to block the winds, violent blizzards occur, making it impossible to travel or leave shelter. Complete calm is rare. The north wind is almost always blowing.

Everything that lives in the Arctic has adapted to the climate remarkably. Over the centuries, the culture of the Eskimos was molded by the demanding conditions of the environment and their way of life was interwoven with the patterns of life in the Arctic.

The Eskimo Way of Life

There are few regions of the earth where people's daily lives have been influenced so much by the changing seasons. Here the people followed a cycle of hunting possibilities offered at different times of the year. Animal habits, plant growth, variations in amount of light, changes in temperature, and the appearance and disapperance of ice and snow regulated their food, clothing, and shelter as well as their social lives.

In early winter many people gathered in large settlements of snowhouses along the shore. Camps were made on the sea ice since a hunter could not travel safely more than a few miles from the settlement in winter, and seal hunting was the main winter activity

for most of the Central Eskimos. Seals were important
not only for winter food: with the coming of severe
cold, seal blubber was needed as fuel. Seals feed fairly
close to the shore and must come up through the ice
floes to get air. When the sea was frozen, Eskimos
hunted seals at these breathing holes.

Dogs could sniff out the small holes hidden under a
cover of snow. A hole searcher, a curved antler rod, was
put down the hole to see if it had been recently used by
a seal. Each seal has a number of holes that it can come
to in order to breathe throughout the day. If a hole
looked promising, the hunter prepared for a long wait.
He built a windbreak of snow blocks and a snow-block
seat that he covered with a fur; then he wrapped his

feet in skins. He placed his harpoon by his side on two rests and put his knife in the snow within easy reach. Then he pushed a seal indicator down the hole — a thin, pointed rod of bone with sinew cord tied through an opening at the top.

When the seal appeared at the breathing hole, it touched the indicator. As soon as the indicator rose up, the hunter thrust his harpoon through the center of the hole as hard as he could. The Eskimo harpoon was a remarkable weapon. The barbed harpoon head came off the shaft as it struck the seal and turned so it could not easily slip out. It had a strong line attached to it. The animal put up a fight under water while the hunter struggled to hold on to the cord. The hunter cut the

18

breathing hole larger and dragged the seal up to the surface. This method worked well in the Arctic because good light was not necessary — the seal indicator could be watched even in the winter twilight. But prolonged blizzards made any hunting impossible, and people often had to live off their stores of food. Many times they were close to starvation.

As days lengthened in springtime and lanes of open water started to form, people began to scatter. Seals and walruses came out of the water to bask in the sun. Now hunting methods changed. The hunter would lie on his stomach and wriggle toward the seals, imitating a seal's movements. The only way a hunter could get close enough to hunt was to make them think he was another seal. He sometimes wore a sealskin cap and used a scratcher to make noises like a seal. When he was in range, he harpooned or clubbed his prey. In some places women were very skillful at this kind of hunting.

Sometimes a small snowhouse was built, only big enough for one man to crouch inside. Bait was placed on the roof, which had a small hole in it. When a sea gull landed, the man inside would grab its legs.

The breakup of the ice and the release from winter brought different kinds of hunting activities. Snow-

houses were abandoned and tents were pitched. In some areas whales reappeared, and seals and walruses could be hunted in the open waters from kayaks. When a seal raised its head above water the hunter threw his spear or shot it with his bow and arrow, then paddled toward it as fast as he could to harpoon it. This was often more successful when several hunters worked together. Seal blubber was stored in hide bags for future needs. The Eskimos placed these precious supplies in pits on the shore piled over with rocks.

BELUGA WHALE

Musk oxen were hunted then too. When attacked, bull musk oxen formed a circle around their calves and females. Dogs kept them at bay while the Eskimos shot arrows at a particular animal until they could get in close enough to kill it with a heavy spear. Rather than haul huge animal carcasses, they often made storage caches near the place where the animal was killed. They could return to these depots during the winter.

Sometimes polar bears might be taken in spring when they were pursuing young seals. Dogs kept the bear at bay until the hunter could make the kill. These were very strong and fierce animals, far more dangerous to hunt than the slow-moving musk ox.

By midsummer the snow cover melted and low-growing vegetation appeared. Many Eskimos left the sea to pursue more profitable land hunting. Caribou moved

CARIBOU

northward toward their summer feeding grounds of mosses, lichens, and small shrubs, which now covered the tundra. Some Eskimos moved inland seeking the herds of caribou. There was some individual hunting, but for the most part group hunting was most successful. Scattered families united again in summer camps near the migration routes of the caribou. Caribou were hunted with spears or with bows and arrows. Bows were made of several pieces of antler tied together; their joints were strengthened with sealskin and they were strung with twisted sinew cord. Sometimes women and children drove the caribou into a lake or river where the men were concealed in their kayaks. The hunters paddled rapidly into the swimming herd, killing as many as they could. Summer was also the time to get wood for sleds, weapons, and other equipment, and sometimes the Eskimos journeyed a hundred miles or more.

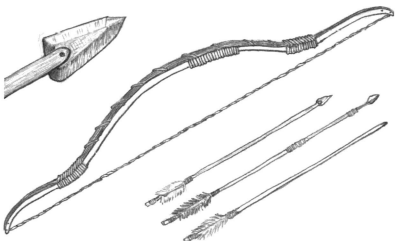

Many birds, geese, and ducks migrate to the Arctic to nest and feed their young on the vast swarms of insects that hatch in the summer. This was a good time for catching birds and gathering eggs. Many kinds of snares were used for catching birds or the birds were struck with a light spear propelled by a spear-thrower. Sometimes Eskimos caught birds just by throwing stones at them. They also had many ingenious traps for catching hares, wolves, and other smaller game.

Summer fishing was an important source of food for many groups, and many people set up camps near a river. Sometimes there were such huge numbers of fish that Eskimos could spear them from the water. Weirs were built at the mouth of a river just below the high-water mark. These were large stone dams with a narrow opening for the fish to get in. The fish entered at high water, but at low water they could not get out. The trapped fish were speared with a leister. This was a long

wooden shaft with two prongs of musk-ox horn tied to
the end. Sharp points of bear bone were inserted in
each prong and on the shaft between them. With this
special tool, fish could be speared quickly and few
slipped away. There were usually enough fish to dry
some for the winter. To store them, two or three men
built an oval cache of large boulders. They covered the
floor with gravel and piled the fish neatly inside. This
was covered with heavy stones pressing directly on the

fish. Foxes and other animals would raid these caches if they were not constructed with great care. In a good year a family would fill three to five caches each containing about five hundred pounds of fish.

In the late summer and early fall, plants and berries became ripe and ready for women and children to gather. They carefully collected grasses for weaving into baskets and boot liners and vegetable material to make lamp wicks, to insulate sleeping platforms, and to add to the soup pot.

As winter approached vast herds of caribou moved south again. This was an important hunting time, a time to store meat for the winter. And at this time the hair of the caribou was best for making into clothing. A family of four needed about thirty skins: seven for the man's clothing, six for the woman's, three or four per child, and the rest for sleeping rugs, platform covers, sledge covers, tents, and other purposes.

Preparing for winter was a very busy time. Women had to sew all the warm clothing. Men needed to make or repair the sledges that were their means of travel over the winter ice. Fish were caught through holes in the ice when the lakes had frozen over in autumn. Often the whole famly would fish together. Since Eskimos believed that all activities associated with hunting on land must be kept entirely separate from sea hunting activities, the sewing of caribou skins had to be finished before they could move to warm igloos in their winter camp and begin seal hunting.

In good times the Eskimos returned to the shore with an abundant supply of food. In the early winter, there was often some leisure time for festivals and visiting friends and relatives.

The seasonal phases and availability of animal and plant life varied from place to place in the Arctic. The cycle of activities varied from group to group. In some areas people moved to the coast in the autumn and made winter homes on the sea ice. For other people autumn was the time to move from the coast to inland winter settlements. The people of each region were hunting and doing the work that was most productive at that season.

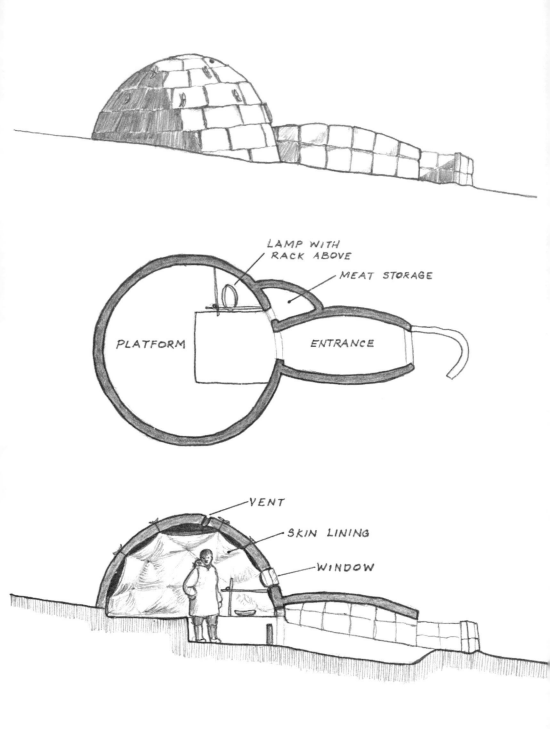

LAMP WITH
RACK ABOVE

MEAT STORAGE

PLATFORM

ENTRANCE

VENT

SKIN LINING

WINDOW

The Igloo

CHAPTER TWO

Igloo Construction

The snow igloo was one of the best dwellings during the Arctic winter and the best shelter for winter travel. A lone traveler with only his regular tool kit could quickly construct a snug shelter almost anywhere, in any weather conditions. The name "igloo" comes from the Eskimo word *iglu,* which is used for any kind of house. Many Eskimos never saw a snow igloo and some groups only used them as temporary shelters while traveling. For the Central Eskimos in Canada it was the most important winter dwelling for centuries. Without the snowhouse, winter survival in that region would have been nearly impossible.

Winter homes were used for about half the year, from October or November until April or May. Although igloos could be constructed by one man alone, they were generally built with the help of women and children or by two or more men working together. Some women could build snowhouses, but it was generally regarded as a man's job.

Villages were usually built on sea ice so as to be close to the source of food. Eskimos tried to find the most sheltered sites for their igloos and villages, using snow ridges or cliffs as a windbreak whenever possible.

The best snow for building a snowhouse was formed in the same drift. Snow formed in layers was likely to split between the layers. If the snow was too hard, it was difficult to cut, and the blocks of snow would not bind together. But it could not be too soft or the blocks would fall apart. Snow that came in contact with sea ice crumbled too easily and had the consistency of sugar, but the top part of drifts that formed on sea ice often could be used.

To test the snow, Eskimos used a snow probe — a straight, thin piece of bone, wood, or antler about one-half inch thick with a band around the tip. If a snow probe was not available, they used something else — a harpoon shaft, knife, or rod of some kind — and put a piece of ice on the tip. The man pushed the probe slowly into the snow drift. If it went down smoothly, the snow was likely to be uniform and firm — good house-building material. If it went down with a series of jerks, the snow was not suitable. Frequently, good snow was only a few yards away from bad snow, so it was often

BONE SNOW PROBE

worthwhile to test a drift that looked promising in several places. It was also important to test that a sufficient quantity of good snow was available. An area about equal to the intended size of the house and about three feet deep was needed.

Finding enough good snow determined where an igloo could be built since it was not possible to carry the blocks of snow very far. Some builders marked a circle on the snow, but experienced builders did not need this to guide them. It was difficult to judge the size the finished igloo would be by the circle marked on the ground. The house was usually much larger than expected, and it took some practice to make allowance for this in planning. The size of the house depended on how many people would be living in it, how much fuel was available, and how long they would stay in it. A good size house for four or five people was between nine and twelve feet in diameter and seven to nine feet high.

The builder used a snow knife to cut the blocks of snow. Men always carried a snow knife with them. Early

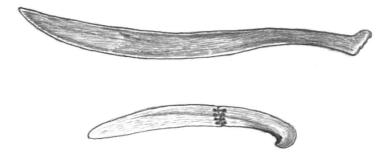

snow knives were made of caribou antler or ivory with indentations in the handle so that they could be gripped firmly. If a long enough single piece was not available, the blade was attached to the handle with bone rivets and sinew thread. After contact with Europeans, iron blades were used, but Eskimos preferred to attach their own handles, which had to be long enough to grip with both hands. The blade was eight to twelve inches long and one or two inches wide. The builder wore a pair of mittens, which tied over the sleeves of his jacket, to keep his hands warm and dry as he worked. Making an igloo

was very hard work, and the builder usually kept quite warm even in the most severe weather conditions.

First the builder marked two parallel lines in the snow as far apart as the desired length of each block — usually between two feet and three and a half feet long. As the blocks were cut out, this space would become the entrance passage to the igloo, so the builder would place this opening facing south, away from the direction of the wind. If he built the igloo on a sloping snow bank, the parallel lines marking the entrance passage would point downhill.

To form an even working surface for cutting the building blocks and to make removal of the first ones easier, the builder cut a wedge-shaped block with his

snow knife. He removed and discarded this block. Then
he cut out building blocks between the parallel lines.
The blocks were one to two feet deep and between four
and six inches thick. These blocks were not quite rectangular; the cuts made between the parallel lines were
slightly curved, corresponding to the curve of the
house. The builder stood in the trough he was forming
as he cut out blocks and kicked lightly at the bottom of
each block to loosen it.

When ten or twelve blocks had been accumulated,
one of them was jammed back into the trough where

the wall of the igloo was intended. Later the doorway would be cut in this block. Then a layer of blocks was arranged in a circle above it, forming the circumference of the igloo. As the builder put the blocks in place, he shaped them with his snow knife so that they would lean in slightly. The last block needed to be fitted carefully in order to make the circle secure.

After this the builder stayed inside the circle, cutting his blocks and building from within. He did not place the next layer of blocks directly on top of the circle. He cut away part of two blocks with a diagonal cut upwards

35

A LEFT-HANDED ESKIMO
IS BUILDING THIS IGLOO

from the bottom corner of one to the top corner of the other. A right-handed person cut from right to left; a left-handed person cut from left to right.

The next block was positioned on the triangular block formed by this cut with its long edge sloping upwards. From then on the blocks continued in a spiral, each block resting on the one beneath it and the one next to it. As more blocks were needed, they were cut from inside the igloo. After a block was in place, the builder passed his snow knife up and down between it and the blocks it touched. This softened the snow at the seams just enough to make them bind.

36

Each block was made to lean in a little more than the previous one. As the spiral continued, the circle became increasingly smaller and the blocks needed to be cut in the shape of trapezoids. The igloo looked as though it should fall in, but a well-built igloo was stable at all stages of construction, and blocks of snow would stick in positions that seemed impossible. The upper blocks were almost horizontal but rested firmly and securely. When completed, the igloo could support a man's weight, and children liked to climb up and slide down the rounded houses.

When there was not enough room for another full

block, the builder cut the remaining hole to an oblong shape. He cut the final block or key block slightly larger than the opening. He pushed this block to the outside through the hole by its shorter edge and turned it into position. Then, while still inside the igloo, he trimmed the edges until the key block fit snugly into position.

Near the center of this block, he cut a hole about two inches across with his snow knife. This would serve as a chimney. It was important to make this opening away from the sides of the block because some melting would take place around the chimney. If the seams melted, the

block would become loose. If there was a very strong
wind, the builder might make the chimney in the center
of one of the upper blocks on the side away from the
direction of the wind.

The builder saved a large block to be used for the
door. An average house required thirty to forty blocks.
There was usually enough snow inside the house to cut
all the blocks. Often there was enough snow so that he
could cut all the blocks and still leave a ledge to form
the platform. If not, he built a large platform inside the
igloo at the back, opposite the door. He placed a row of

low blocks across the igloo floor and shoveled snow into the space behind them. He packed the snow of the platform to make it firm. The floor was stamped level and smooth. The platform took up about two-thirds of the interior and was two and a half to three feet high.

Usually snow was left on each side of the entrance passage, where it was difficult to cut good blocks. The builder made one of these ledges into a table for the stone lamp. The other area provided snow that could be melted for drinking water. Finally he cut a small doorway in the entrance passage below the igloo and crawled out.

There was still outside work to be done. Often his wife or a companion was helping him, and this work was done while the man worked from the inside. Sometimes, when building a large house, two men worked together, one man cutting the blocks and handing them to the builder. But in a small house or temporary shelter, the two would get in each other's way. It was more helpful for one to do the outside work. The outside of the igloo needed chinking — filling in gaps between blocks by pressing in soft snow. Sometimes the house was banked to help stop the wind from blowing out the chinking and to make the house warmer. This was done by shoveling snow over the igloo. Snow shovels were made from an antler frame with a piece of sealskin fastened by sinew, or from wood with a bone handle.

If a house had to be built when a very strong wind was blowing, Eskimos first made a shelter wall of strong blocks and constructed the igloo behind it. This prevented blocks from being blown down or blown to pieces. Sometimes a wall was put up around a house after it was completed to protect it in severe storms.

An experienced Eskimo builder could construct a small temporary igloo in about one hour. A larger, more elaborate house intended for longer use was built very carefully and took more time to complete.

Necessities and Comforts

When the house was completed, the women came in and arranged the living quarters. Furnishings and belongings were often brought in through a hole in the wall rather than through the low doorway. Then the hole was closed up again.

The stone lamp fueled with seal oil was the most important fixture in the igloo. It provided heat and bright light and also served as a stove and a clothes drier. It burned quietly without much draft and therefore brought in little cold air. The lamp was a shallow oval tray hollowed from soft soapstone. It had a flat bottom and raised sides. Eskimos often traveled great distances or traded with other groups for soapstone. Making soapstone utensils was hard work and took a long time. The work was usually done by the man, but when the piece was completed, he gave it to his wife and it became her permanent property. A broken utensil would be repaired rather than replaced.

Lamps varied in size. A hunter or traveler would carry along a small lamp, twelve to fifteen inches long. For a permanent family igloo, the lamp was between twenty and thirty inches long. Occasionally a large ceremonial igloo had a lamp forty inches long. The width was about half the length. Wicks were made from moss or cotton grass. The flame was regulated by how much of the wick was immersed in the oil. It could be a low

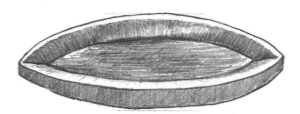

flame for a night light or a high flame for cooking. A housewife prided herself on keeping a lamp with a bright, clear flame that never smoked.

The housewife usually made the fire by striking pyrite against a piece of flint or iron and letting the sparks fall on dry moss. Pyrite is a mineral that looks very much like gold. A kind of drill was sometimes used to start fires: a stick with a point of hard willow was rotated rapidly in a driftwood board and as soon as smoke appeared, the tinder — usually dried moss — was put at the point.

Sometimes some blubber was hung over the lamp. As the fuel level in the lamp grew low, the wick became longer and burned higher. Then the blubber above would begin to melt and drip into the lamp. The fuel

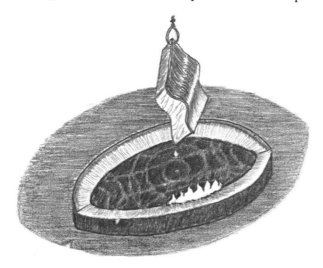

level would rise, the wick would be short again, and the blubber would stop melting. In this way the lamp could be left burning without much attention.

Once the lamp was lit, the woman fixed a frame for hanging her cooking pot or tea kettle over the flame. Cooking pots were carved from a single block of soapstone. They were usually rectangular, between twelve and twenty-four inches long, with straight sides and holes for suspending cords. Cooking was slow over this kind of stove, but it suited the Eskimos' needs. They stewed their meat slowly, adding what was at hand to the pot.

Above the cooking frame the woman set a rack for drying damp clothes. This was a wooden ring with an irregular network of sinew thongs supported by three sticks. One stick was placed upright in the snow of the lamp table while the other two were pushed into the walls at right angles to each other and tied to the top of

44

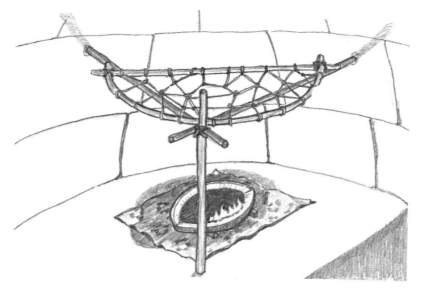

the upright support. Clothes or boots could be hung overnight on this tray of netting to be ready in the morning. Cooking utensils and equipment for tending the lamp were arranged nearby on the table.

When the kitchen area was in order, the woman went to work on the living and sleeping area. First she fixed a piece of wood along the edge of the platform to prevent it from wearing down and breaking off. Then an insulating material was spread on the platform to keep moisture away from the bedding. The woman used the best material she had available — mountain heather, moss, willow twigs, caribou ribs, or grasses. This was covered with skins of caribou or bear, making a dry, comfortable place to sit and sleep. The family slept with their heads toward the door using their clothing as pillows. They did not wear anything in bed. They used warm fur blankets or sleeping bags. The woman slept with her head opposite the lamp so that she could tend to it in the night without getting up.

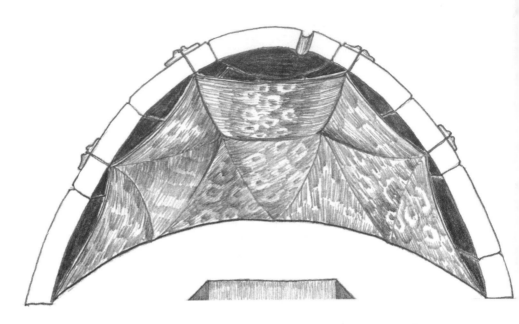

For permanent houses, Eskimos used a lining suspended from the roof. The lining was made of skins sewn together, usually sealskin with the hair side toward the interior of the house. Often they used worn-out tent skins. The lining was hung by sinew cords that went through the walls and were tied to pegs on the outside. The bottom edge of the lining was pegged down to the platform on the inside. A large air space was left between the top of the lining and the roof of the igloo. With the lining in place and the air exit hole, there was always cool air between the lining and the interior wall of the igloo. The living space could be kept warmer without melting the igloo. This also prevented dripping.

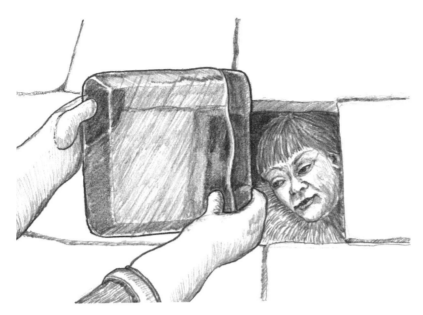

Eskimos put in a window above the entrance to the igloo. It was made from fresh-water ice three or four inches thick or from a piece of gut-skin. Gut-skin gave more light than ice and was easier to wipe clean of frost but was not as airtight. The window was usually a rectangle or a trapezoid. When frost collected on the window, the woman scraped it off with her all-purpose knife.

While the woman arranged the inside of the house, the man worked on the entrance passage and any adjoining structures. These varied with the family's needs. Sometimes a long tunnel was built as a windbreak. This tunnel was only about three and a half feet high and three feet wide, although it might be ten to twenty feet long.

Often there was a storage room in front of the main living area. In front of that there was sometimes a room in which the dogs could stay during bad weather. These were usually smaller, dome-shaped houses connected to the main house. Among some people they were vaulted like tunnels. The entrance at the very outer tunnel had a sharp angled turn to keep out the wind.

Eskimos usually constructed a cache beside the igloo. This was a place to store their food and harnesses. Outer clothing could also be left in the cache when the family went into the house for the night. Bundles of extra clothing, tools, and utensils were arranged around the walls, but igloos were rather small, and Eskimos did not crowd them with things not needed inside. The cache was built of three walls of snow blocks, with the igloo forming the fourth wall. It was high enough to

keep everything out of reach of dogs and other animals. Harnesses and clothing were made from animal skins, and these animals would eat them if they were hungry. Small houses were sometimes built for a dog and her puppies. A separate small enclosure was often built for a toilet.

If there was not oil available for fuel, a separate cookhouse might be built off the passageway. The smoke from any other fuel — wood, moss, caribou tallow — was very objectionable inside the house. The Caribou Eskimos, who lived inland and did not have seal oil for heating, lived in unheated igloos. Besides having to endure much lower temperatures in their huts, they could not easily melt snow for fresh drinking water. Instead they kept an ice hole open in a lake or river. Ice had to be scraped and chipped away regularly. Fresh water was scooped out and carried in a skin bucket. Eskimos who lived on sea ice could melt snow or find ice that was old enough to have lost its saltiness. Old ice could be identified by its bluish color.

A man traveling alone built a very small, low house without a platform. One or two blocks were usually placed along the windward side of the entrance passage to prevent snow from drifting into it. A family building a temporary shelter on a journey would not have a storeroom or window and only a shelter wall in front of the entrance. If they were traveling with a lot of belongings, a small separate storage igloo might be constructed.

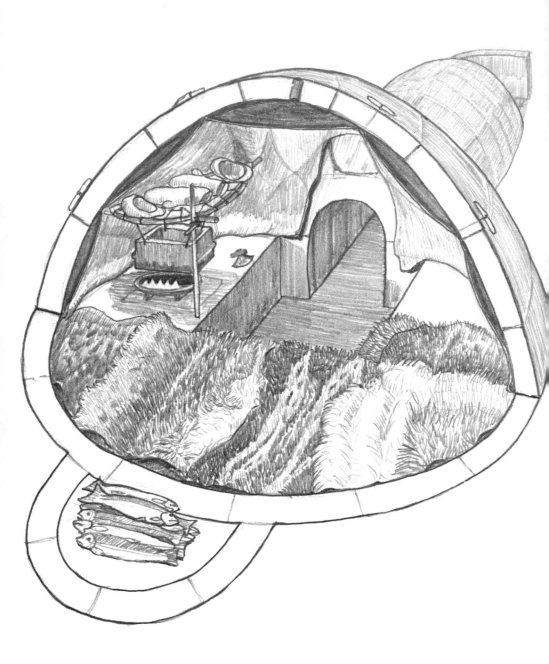

Living in an Igloo

CHAPTER THREE

Shelter from the Arctic

It would be hard to conceive of a better shelter against the Arctic winter than the igloo. The dome shape was well suited to the climate. The igloo was very strong and could withstand violent winds. It exposed the least possible surface area to the wind and cold. It also enclosed a large volume in a small structure. It could house a family comfortably and could be effectively heated by one oil lamp. If fuel was not available, it gave sufficient protection from the elements with only the heat generated by the people living in it.

The igloo was not a hemisphere; a true hemisphere would collapse. An igloo was a catenary. A catenary is the shape of a chain held at both ends. If you could fix the curve of the chain and turn it upright, it would be the

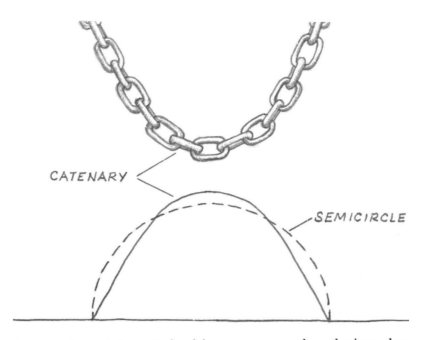

CATENARY

SEMICIRCLE

shape of an igloo. It is this more complex design that enables Eskimos to build these structures without support. As an igloo settled and the snow became compressed, the structure became a bit shorter. But in a hemispherical structure, the sides would buckle and the top would fall in. Eskimos arrived at this form by trial and error. If a man had to build a shelter with snow that was not of good quality, he made it much narrower and taller than usual. He compensated for the less stable material with a more stable form.

Eskimos used the air-capture principle in their houses. The igloo was like an inverted container that trapped the rising warm air. The entrance passage was positioned to slope upward when possible. It tunneled

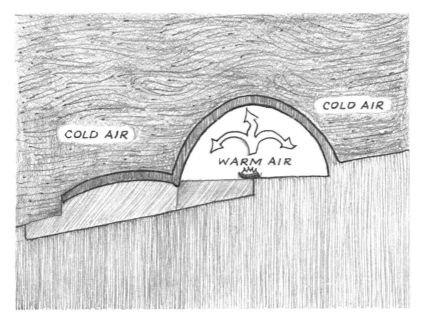

under the wall of the igloo and opened into the living quarters below the sleeping and working area. This helped keep out cold drafts. The platform — the main living space — took advantage of rising warm air.

Although snow may seem to be the least likely material for building a warm, snug house, dry snow has good insulating properties and is an excellent wall material. When the lamp was lit, the inside melted a little and then froze up again, glazing the inside shell with a thin coating of ice. This ice film would seal any tiny openings in the igloo. It also acted like modern aluminum insulation, reflecting heat back into the snowhouse. The inside temperature would average sixty-five degrees higher than the outside air. With a lining, the inside temperature could be raised quite a lot without melting the igloo.

If the house became too cold, the chimney opening could be closed with moss, a piece of skin, or a mitten. Snow was not used, as it made too tight a closing for proper ventilation. If the igloo became too stuffy or too warm, the chimney could be widened to six or eight inches.

The igloo was easy to keep clean. In many cases it was abandoned before refuse and dirt had accumulated. In snowhouses that were used for a long time, the woman cleaned house by scraping a layer from the floor with her all-purpose knife and a shovel. Then she put down a new snow layer in its place.

Snowhouses did leak and lumps of snow were sometimes placed on the roof where it was dripping to stop annoying leaks temporarily. The dry snow would absorb the water like a sponge.

The change from a tent to a warm tight igloo was always a comfort, but snowhouses did not last forever. A snowhouse usually had to be abandoned when most of the wall had turned to ice; it became too cold and dripped all the time. By May it was a less comfortable dwelling. The snow was soft, and holes formed in the roof very readily. Bulges formed that would sink and fall in, getting everything wet. Sometimes igloos could be made to last a little longer by placing a cone of snow at the lowest point. As the snow absorbed the moisture, it dripped off and could be collected. The roof could

sometimes be supported with planks, but this generally meant it was time to move into another kind of dwelling.

Igloos did not need to last long. Hunting conditions forced Eskimos to move often, abandoning their old igloos and building new ones. An igloo was used for an average of one month, but it usually could be made to last as long as it was needed. It did not take long to build and gave excellent protection from a hostile climate while it lasted.

Clothing

Eskimos spent much of their time out of doors, and the design of their clothing was as important as the design of their shelter. Their lives depended upon it. Anyone exposed to the bitter Arctic without adequate clothing was in as much danger as an astronaut without an adequate space suit. Eskimos could survive a severe blizzard without any shelter wearing only a regular winter outfit.

Eskimo clothing was extremely efficient. It was lightweight, comfortable, warm, and allowed the wearer to move around easily. A complete winter outfit weighed only about ten pounds. By contrast, an average Minnesota businessman wears twenty to thirty pounds of clothing on his way to work in winter; if caught in a sudden blizzard, he would be in danger of freezing to death. Getting dressed takes him about fifteen times as long as it took an Eskimo — an important consideration at temperatures below freezing.

Some of the same principles used in their igloos were used in the design of Eskimos' clothing. Eskimo clothing used the air-capture system. It held in the warm air that would ordinarily escape through openings or tiny spaces in the weave of material. Eskimo women made their garments from nonporous animal skins, usually caribou. The air inside the clothing was warmed by body heat. The warm air was trapped inside the almost airtight garment.

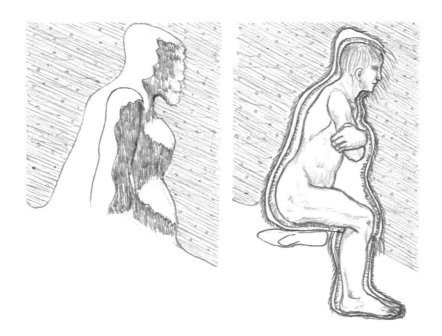

If an Eskimo had to be out in a blizzard, he would sit, not lie down, even when sleeping. In this way, he prevented warm air from escaping around the edge of the coat. If a person was injured or for some reason had to lie flat, the bottom of his coat was tied around him with a cord to hold in the warmth.

Clothing was designed so that the wearer was in an air pocket and his skin was away from the garment. Eskimo clothes were loosely fitted, but snug at the neck and over the shoulders. The fur side was worn inside and air could circulate inside the garment. This also helped to prevent the clothing from absorbing moisture.

Eskimo clothing had an automatic temperature con-

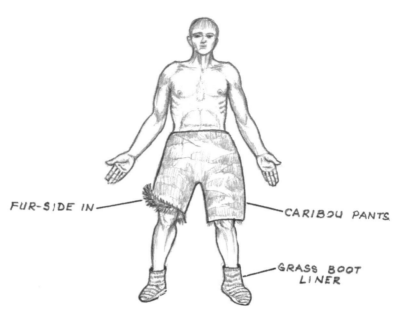

FUR-SIDE IN

CARIBOU PANTS

GRASS BOOT LINER

trol. If the wearer was running or working hard, the fringe of fur around the bottom of his coat would flap, circulating the cold air beneath his jacket. He could also adjust the temperature by pulling out his coat at his chin, releasing some of the warm air. When the wearer was not moving very much and not producing as much body heat, the circulation of air slowed down.

In summer an Eskimo wore a hooded caribou jacket, which went down to about mid-thigh, and caribou pants, both with the fur-side in. The face opening in the hood was only large enough to push it back when it was not needed. The jacket was sometimes fringed to assist in temperature control. For the coldest weather, Eskimos added an extra hooded jacket and pants with

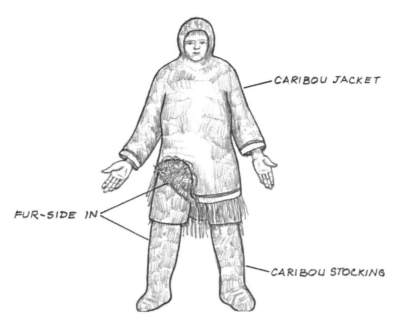

CARIBOU JACKET

FUR-SIDE IN

CARIBOU STOCKING

the fur on the outside. Fur trim of bear or wolverine around the face opening of the hood and the bottom of the jacket helped prevent cold air from getting in and warm air from getting out. The upper part of the sleeves were cut wide so that when they were very cold, Eskimos could slip their arms inside their jackets and take advantage of the heat generated by their bodies. There were no buttons, hooks, lacings, or fastenings of any kind that would let air in or out. Their fur boots were high enough to overlap their pants. The soles were made of the thickest available hides. Boot liners of soft, warm birdskin or woven grass were sometimes added. Mittens were of caribou or bear skin. Men, women, and older children used the same system of clothing.

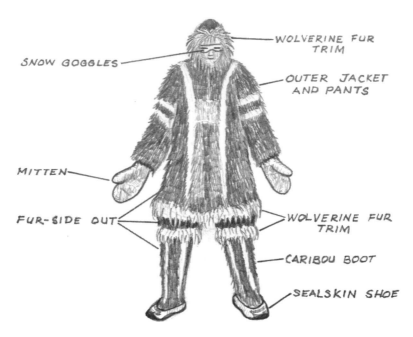

SNOW GOGGLES

WOLVERINE FUR
TRIM

OUTER JACKET
AND PANTS

MITTEN

FUR-SIDE OUT

WOLVERINE FUR
TRIM

CARIBOU BOOT

SEALSKIN SHOE

Preparing caribou skins for clothing was a long, tiring process, occupying both men and women in late autumn and early winter. Skin for clothing had to be dried in the air or over the lamp, scraped with a bone scraper, and twisted and softened with the hands. Then it was sprayed with water, rolled up, and put away for several days. This was followed by several more processes of scraping and stretching the skin and sometimes chewing it until it was very soft and flexible.

Clothes were sewn by women. A woman used her *ulu* to cut the skin without using any pattern. The *ulu* was also called a woman's knife, and it was the most important tool an Eskimo woman owned. It was a multipurpose knife used for cutting and scraping skins,

60

preparing food, chopping lamp moss, cutting sticks of wood, and chopping ice. Most women had several of different sizes for different purposes. An *ulu* had a semicircular blade and a wood or bone handle joined together by a narrow piece of bone or metal.

Clothing was finely stitched with sinew, long pieces of which were taken from each side of a caribou's spine. These were shredded and used for thread. The seamstress used a three-sided needle made of bone or ivory. Eskimo clothes were as beautiful as they were practical. Furs of contrasting colors were worked into the design of the garment, and it was elegantly finished with decorative handiwork using shells, beadwork, and colorful fringes.

Babies traveled naked inside their mother's coats. The infant was supported by a belt and carried at the small of her back. Children old enough to walk wore a single-piece suit that covered hands and feet. There was a hole in the palm so they could uncover their hands when necessary. Short boots were worn with it. They had an inner and outer set of this clothing.

Eskimo clothing needed special care since the skins would harden or decay if they became damp. Garments not being used were stored in skin bags. Before entering the warm snowhouse, Eskimos took off their outer clothes and carefully beat them free of snow with a curved snow-beater, a flat, blunt-edged piece of wood. Damp clothes were put on the drying rack overnight so that they would be dry and comfortable the next morning. In areas without blubber for lamps, the inability to dry clothes was more of a problem than the unheated snowhouse. If clothing did become stiff, women rubbed and chewed it until it was pliable.

Eskimos made goggles to protect their eyes from the glare of snow and ice. These were made of ivory or wood and tied on with thongs. The wearer looked out through narrow slits.

With their clothing system, Eskimos were well protected and could work or play outdoors as easily as people in warmer climates. Well-designed clothing made it possible for people to live in Arctic lands that would otherwise have been uninhabitable.

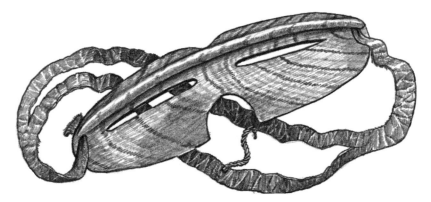

Food

Eskimos lived healthy lives on a diet that consisted almost entirely of meat and fish. They hunted whatever animals were most readily available at that particular season, and no source of meat was overlooked. Although boiled meat was preferred when there was enough fuel, some meat was eaten uncooked. Raw meat gives more energy and nourishment than the same amount of cooked meat. Often Eskimos enjoyed cooked food at the end of the day when they were going to rest after the meal, but ate raw meat while they were active outdoors hunting or traveling.

Eskimos also ate internal organs and animal skins that were not considered edible by the Europeans who came to the Arctic. These people were often horrified by Eskimo eating habits, but many who refused to eat Eskimo food became very sick and some died. Travelers in the Arctic mostly suffered from scurvy, a disease caused by vitamin C deficiency. Internal organs and fresh meat are rich in vitamins. White men who ate an Eskimo diet learned that it could prevent and cure scurvy.

Eskimos would not eat polar bear livers. They believed these should be offered in gratitude for successful hunting and to honor the spirit of the animal killed. Many explorers who did not trust Eskimo wisdom became sick. Modern research has shown that the polar bear's liver can be very poisonous, containing harmful levels of vitamin A.

BELUGA WHALE   WALRUS
HARP SEAL   POLAR BEAR
          ARCTIC CHAR

Eskimos ate a large quantity of meat in times of plenty — four to eight pounds a day. In cold weather and especially when they were traveling, one half of their food was fat. Having to live mainly on lean meat was the same as starving to Eskimos, no matter how large a quantity of lean meat was available. A steady diet of lean meat could cause serious illness or death.

Food was usually cooked by boiling. The large rectangular kettle was placed over the lamp on a four-legged frame or was supported above the lamp by a horizontal pole. Snow or ice was melted in the pot and available food was added to be simmered into a rich stew.

There is very little edible plant life in the Arctic. Berries and wild plants were gathered when available

— bilberries, black crowberries, cloudberries, willow leaves, mountain sorrel leaves, and some roots. These were eaten fresh, mixed with blubber, added to the cooking pot to be boiled with the rest of the meal, or stored for later use. Studies have shown that the plants preferred by nearly all native groups were those with the highest content of important vitamins, and that Eskimo methods of storing and preparing them were excellent for preserving their nutritional value. The white people living in the Arctic generally preferred different species, which we have learned were of less nutritional value. Although plants accounted for only a small quantity of the Eskimo diet, they did provide important vitamins and nutrients. They were a regular part of Eskimo meals when available, and they were considered important enough to be gathered every year. Over the years Eskimos had learned by trial and error which foods were healthful for them.

Families

In the Arctic, with its limited resources, a family was very much on its own. When there was not enough food available to support large numbers of people, families went their separate ways, surviving as best they could. When they formed larger communities, these were really a collection of families. Each family member was important and had specific jobs to do. Families cared deeply about each other, but the welfare of the family as a whole was the most important consideration.

Fathers were highly respected. The life of everyone in the family depended on his hunting skills for food. It was a source of great pride and satisfaction for a man to be known as a good provider for his family, the elderly, and neighbors who were in need. Men were also responsible for transportation. They took care of the sledge and the dog team and made and used the kayak. They made weapons, tools, and utensils, including things used by women. Men built the igloos and put up the tents.

The mother was the center of the family, always busy taking care of the home, preparing food, tending the oil lamp night and day, caring for and playing with the children. She sewed and mended the clothing, bedding, tents, and boat coverings. She did some hunting and fishing and collected plants, berries, and eggs. She was loved and needed.

Children spent their first years close to their mothers, carried against their backs, secure in being loved, cared for, and highly valued. Young children had few responsibilities, but their play often helped them learn skills they would need later on. Boys made hunting implements and used snow sculptures for target practice. Later they practiced hunting small animals. They also sometimes built small playhouses. Girls had dolls or puppies to play with and often sewed small clothing and shoes for their dolls. Often young children were not even required to help carry a pack when traveling. During the times of continuous daylight, children would play outside far into the night hours. As they grew older, they participated in family activities by helping their parents. If children were orphaned, they were adopted by relatives or by a childless family and were accepted as part of that family.

Men and women were rarely idle at home. There was always mending to be done or new things to be made. Visitors often brought their work and kept busy while they chatted. Work was carefully done and many utensils were very beautiful.

Families were very close and each member depended on the others. Although jobs were separated, there were

many times when they needed to help each other. Women helped with hunting and housebuilding when they were needed. If a woman was very busy with sewing, her husband would help. Survival depended on families working together.

Eskimos believed in a spirit world. Animals, hills, streams, and all things in nature had souls. Angry spirits could cause hard times. Being killed by a crudely made weapon might offend an animal's spirit, which would warn his brother animals of the hunter's disrespect. When a seal was killed, the hunter's wife poured fresh water in the seal's mouth, hoping that its soul would tell other seals and that they would want to be caught for the chance to drink fresh, clear water. When the family moved out of a tent or house, they lifted the back of the tent or broke through the back of the snowhouse. They believed that by doing this they could trick any bad spirit trying to follow them to their new house.

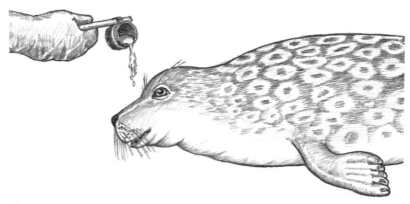

Games and Pastimes

Igloos usually rang with laughter and fun. It was especially important to have ways of passing the time during the long weeks of darkness. During the dark days time passed slowly. Storms and blizzards put a stop to all hunting, and often it was not safe to venture outdoors at all. Eskimos ate and slept, talked and told stories, and danced and played games.

In the summer, when the sun shone all night long, people did not feel like sleeping and games continued happily. Children played make-believe. Boys had toy sledges, bows and arrows, kayaks, and harpoons. Girls played with dolls of ivory, wood, or caribou skin stuffed with hair. They had small lamps, *ulus*, cooking utensils, and cooking pots. Fathers carved small ice toys for their

children. Children spent a lot of time playing outside. Girls sometimes had story knives, which they used to draw pictures in the snow illustrating the story they were telling. They could smooth over one picture and draw the next.

There were many games for grown-ups as well as children. In one game they tried to catch a piece of bone with holes in it on a stick. The bone was attached to the stick by a cord. Different holes had different values. In another game a piece of bone with holes in it was hung from the roof. At the signal all players would strike at the holes with a stick. The winner was the one who got his stick in the hole. Sometimes a knife was laid on the platform and spun around. The person the knife

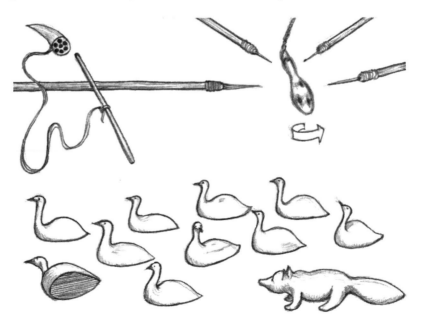

pointed at would have to perform a task set by the others. Eskimos played different kinds of gambling games. They also liked competitive games — wrestling, tug-of-war, jumping over ropes, and ball games. Cat's cradle was a favorite Eskimo game, and they made complex string figures representing animals, hunters, spirits, and familiar things in their lives. Dancing was one of their greatest pleasures. There were masked dances and dances performed with a drum. Dances frequently brightened the long, dark winter days.

Snow Villages

CHAPTER FOUR

Settlements

Eskimos lived a roaming life, but they followed a pattern in their movements. Groups had places to which they returned every year and formed settlements for larger, cooperative hunting ventures. People got together to socialize and trade and for ceremonies and dances. For the Central Eskimos, summer settlements were groups of tents; winter villages were clusters of snow huts.

In winter villages, connected igloos were sometimes built to be shared by several families. These would have two or more snowhouses, storage rooms, and a dog shelter with one common exit. People could go from house to house and room to room without going outside. Large igloos housing more than one family often had two platforms. These could connect with smaller houses in one snow block.

There was often a large dance house in the village

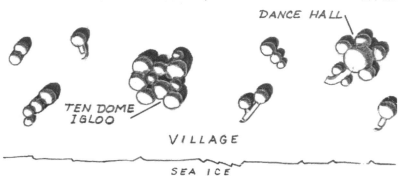

that served as a meeting place for singing, dancing, feasting, and ceremonies. Sometimes two large connected snowhouses were built with platforms, one for the men and one for the women. Dances were performed under the arch joining the two houses. In some

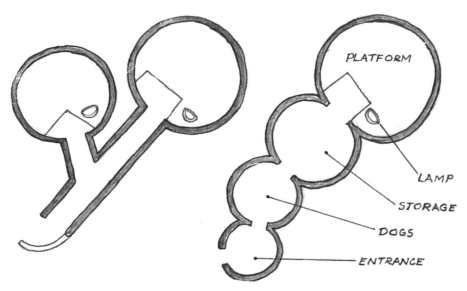

DANCE
HALL

COOK HOUSE

TEN DOME IGLOO

areas the festivals or dances were held in one large igloo. This usually had no platform; men stood on one side and women on the other. The lamp was on a block of snow in the middle. Several family dwellings might be built around the large meeting chamber opening into it.

Many of the activities in the dance house were held for the enjoyment of socializing with friends. People got together for informal singing, dancing, contests, and fun. Sometimes dancers wore comic masks and held contests, trying to make each other laugh. A storyteller would promise to tell a story no one had ever heard to the end and stretch the tale out until his audience had fallen asleep.

The dance house was also a place for artistic performances. Eskimos lived in an environment where life was a constant struggle to meet basic needs, but art was one of those needs. Creating beautiful tools, utensils, and clothing was important. Their music, dancing, singing, and storytelling also filled a creative need. Some of the dances had fixed motions that were rehearsed and carefully performed. Other songs and dances were improvised for a particular occasion. The stories and legends spun by storytellers to fill the endless winter nights formed the oral tradition passed on from generation to generation. A good story or song eventually spread from one village to another throughout the Arctic.

The plan of a settlement varied every time it was built. When families rebuilt igloos at another site or

76

when they reassembled the next season, they built houses that were as simple or as elaborate as they needed at that particular time.

Community Life

Eskimos thought of themselves as part of a village. Villages had traditional territories where they hunted. They varied in size from about thirty to five hundred people. The settlement needed enough people for hunting ventures that required cooperation, and enough people to survive disasters. But the land could not support too large a community. A number of these villages dotted the shores about ten to thirty miles apart. Visiting, trading, and socializing among villages was fairly frequent.

Large settlements united people who had been separated for a long time. There were always stories and gossip to be shared when the people got together. Women were in and out of each other's igloos during the day. The whole community came out to greet the hunters on their return, to see how successful they had been and to hear the accounts of the hunt.

In the igloo hunters told of their deeds, acting out the dangers and how they had faced them. In addition to providing lively conversation, gatherings where people could tell the stories of their hunting experiences were good places for sharing information. Eskimos always wanted to learn as much as they could, and they listened carefully as their fellow hunters told of their experiences. Hunters shared information they had heard from other people as well as their own personal observations. The body of knowledge of the group was always being enlarged and improved in this way. Eskimos were always able to find humor in mistakes and misfortunes. Things often went wrong, and Eskimos knew that anger never helped. Hunters never tired of recounting their most frustrating errors and laughing about them with their friends.

Sharing was an important part of survival in the Arctic. Eskimos worked out meat-sharing arrangements so that everyone got a fair share of food. Each hunter had a partner for sharing a particular part of the animal. The hunter always gave the seal's flipper to his flipper-partner, who would do the same when he had a successful hunt. Partners were appointed at the time of a young man's first kill. Giving gifts of food to widows, elderly, or needy people brought good luck to the hunter. Eskimos were willing to share what they had with someone who was not a good hunter as long as they did not think he was lazy.

Each family in the village made what it needed. Individuals might become known as experts in a certain technique — best knife maker, fastest seamstress, or most skillful walrus hunter. But people did not specialize in one particular activity. Everyone needed to be versatile and able to do many jobs.

There was no formal government in these villages. They did not have chiefs or councils to regulate activities. Leaders of hunting parties were chosen because they had skills and abilities that were needed at the time. The leaders rarely gave orders and always consulted the other hunters. Individuals who were respected for their wisdom might be called on for help and advice in community matters.

A shaman was perhaps the most influential person in the community. He was believed to have supernatural

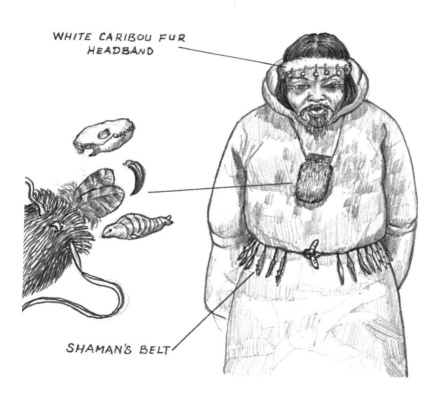

WHITE CARIBOU FUR HEADBAND

SHAMAN'S BELT

SHAMAN'S MASK

powers and was often more feared than respected. People consulted shamans to find out when bad weather would stop, where lost articles could be found, when animals were best hunted, or when strangers would come. The shaman would evoke spirits to cure sickness, give strength to a hunter, or help the community. People also came to shamans when they were angry at someone and wanted revenge.

Eskimos had many taboos, things that were forbidden because they were believed to be dangerous. Many of these restrictions were made by the shamans. Some were handed down for generations and applied to all people; others applied only to a particular situation. A sick person might not be allowed to eat certain foods just because the shaman ordered it, not for any medical reasons. Taboos were enforced by threats of bad luck or sickness.

One of the most important spirits to Eskimos was Sedna. She lived at the bottom of the sea and controlled the sea animals. When she was angry, she sent storms or kept the seals and walruses with her. When animals became scarce, the shaman would go into a trance. He would communicate with Sedna to find out what had angered her and what the people must do to make her release the animals again.

Daily life in the Arctic was full of dangers. Eskimos faced many hardships that were beyond their control. Many people carved ivory figures to carry with them for luck in hunting. Any charms or ceremonies that might bring good luck were useful and important to them. Villagers held dances and ceremonies in the large dance house to honor the spirits of the animals they hunted.

Traveling in the Arctic

CHAPTER FIVE

Land Travel

Traveling was an important part of Eskimo life. Even when they settled in one place for some time, men needed to make journeys to find game. These journeys might last several days. Eskimo families also made trips to visit relatives or friends, stopping along the way if the hunting was good. Time was not important; they arrived at their destination sooner or later.

In some regions the sea was covered with ice for nine or ten months of the year. There were open waters for only a short period every year, and even then water travel was difficult because of the dangerous drift ice. Most journeys were made over land. During the brief time when there was no snow, Eskimos traveled on foot with people and dogs carrying the supplies. A good dog could easily carry twenty to twenty-five pounds; they often carried much more than that. Eskimos also carried heavy burdens on these journeys.

For most of the year, the dog sledge was the most important means of land transportation. The sledge traveled well over ice and snow, and it could sometimes be used on smooth tundra in the summer. The sledge was built of wood, whalebone, or whatever material was at hand. If none of these materials was available, some Eskimos made sledges out of old sealskin tent covers. The tent sheet was softened by lowering it into river waters through a hole in the ice. The wet skin was spread flat and cut in half. Fish were laid along one side of each half. (Frozen fish often served as a substitute for wood in an emergency.) Then each piece was rolled very tightly with the fish inside to add thickness and bound with sealskin thongs. The ends were turned up, and these runners were left to freeze solid. Crossbars made of caribou antlers were fastened to the runners

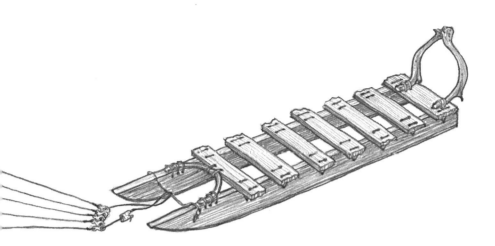

with hide thongs. The handles for guiding the sledge were usually made of caribou antler. Sledges were five to fifteen feet long.

Shoeing the runners of the sledge was an important and time-consuming job. It protected the runners and kept them from sticking in the snow. Most Eskimos used a mud shoeing. They thawed mud and moss, removing any stones and lumps. This mud was mixed with water and kneaded to an even consistency. Then they shaped the mixture into balls about the size of a fist, laid them along the runners, and spread the mud evenly with their hands. When the mud had frozen, it was smoothed with a knife. This was then topped with an ice shoeing. They sprayed mouthfuls of water onto a piece of bear skin and rubbed the wet fur over the frozen mud until there was a hard, even coating of ice as smooth as glass. The smooth ice would glide easily over soft powdery snow. The whole process of shoeing took several hours.

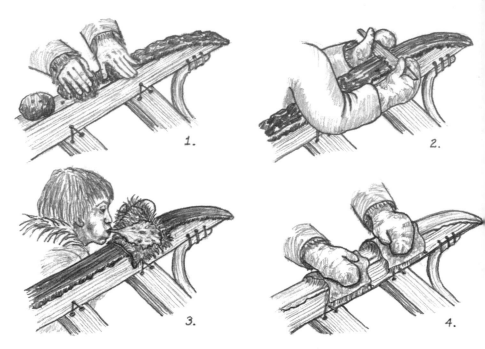

Ice fields were never a smooth plain. Heavy winds and blizzards pitted the surface of the ice and left hard, uneven snow drifts. Strong sea currents underneath would push up great ridges of ice. Huge broken blocks of ice formed impassable barriers. Shoeing was often damaged on a journey, and it had to be repaired or replaced right away. Eskimo travelers carried water pouches in their coats so they could repair the ice shoeing at any time.

If no sledge was available or if the snow was too soft to use a sledge, Eskimos harnessed the dogs to a caribou or bear skin and hauled whatever needed to be transported on this improvised sledge without runners.

Dogs had harnesses and traces made of hide. The

dogs were harnessed to the sled in a fanlike formation. The lead dog was on the longest strap in the middle. The other dogs were on each side, those with the shortest straps on the outside. This formation was preferred by most Eskimos because each dog pulled an equal share of the load and each could pick his way through the irregularities in the snow. All dogs could be released at once from the sledge and from each other in case of attack by a bear or another animals. If one dog fell into a snowdrift, the others were not dragged in and could help pull out the fallen dog.

Dogs had the best traction for travel in the Arctic. Training and handling the dog team required great skill and strength. Women frequently helped and were often as good at driving as the men. One dog became the clear leader of the team. He was usually the strongest and most spirited. He got the choice pieces of food, broke up fights among the other dogs, and kept unruly dogs under control. Dogs had to be well-trained to keep them from eating the meat they were hauling, clothing and equipment made from animals, and even their own harnesses. A family usually owned four to six dogs. Teams of more than ten were rare, as it was often difficult to supply enough food for a larger team. If the load was very heavy, the family would help pull the sledge. The dog sledge moved in a whirl of flying snow, and the air was made white with frost. The sledge bounced and clattered over the rough ice, winding its way through crystal mazes formed by the ice and snow.

Water Travel

The kayak was developed for the times when hunting could best be done on open waters. It was a very efficient vessel for hunting seals and walruses. At one time there were probably two different kinds of kayaks: one for hunting caribou on lakes and rivers and one for hunting sea animals. The two kinds were important because of the Eskimo belief that the things used for hunt-

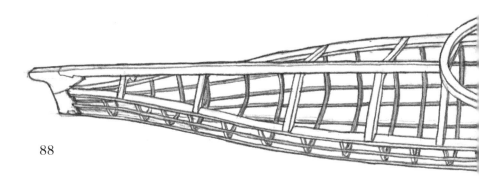

ing land animals and sea animals should be kept separate. The two kayaks did not vary greatly in form, and by later times only one kind of kayak was in use.

The frame was made of driftwood or whalebone and willow branches. It was entirely covered with sealskins except for an oval-shaped opening where the hunter sat. It took six or seven sealskins to make a cover. To

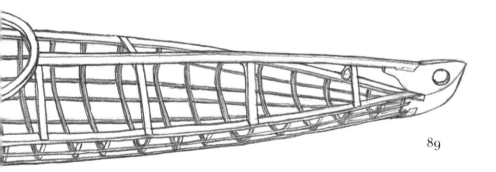

attach the cover to the frame, the Eskimos wet the skin cover, laid it out, and placed the kayak skeleton in the middle. The skin was pulled up and around it and brought together. Using a zigzag stitch, the sinew was gradually pulled tighter and tighter until the edges were together and the cover taut. A kayak was long and narrow for easy handling. It was about twenty to twenty-five feet long, nineteen inches wide, and ten inches deep; it weighed fifty to sixty pounds.

The kayaker fitted in like part of the boat. He wore a special waterproof suit made of gut skin. He drew the skin at the opening of the kayak tightly around his waist with a belt, and he and his kayak were watertight from one end to the other. The hunter used a double paddle to steer the kayak. If he tipped over, he could bring himself up again. The sealskin cover had rests and thongs to hold his hunting equipment.

In some areas there was more open water for longer periods of time. When people had to travel over water, they used the umiak. It was also used for hunting large whales. This kind of boat was used more frequently in Alaska and Greenland. It was known as the "woman's boat" because women manipulated the large paddles while men steered. The umiak was skin covered, but wide and open. It was thirty to thirty-five feet long and could carry several families along with their belongings. It looked fragile but it was springy and could withstand ice or rocks better than a wooden boat. Holes could be patched quite easily with a piece of sealskin. Sometimes

90

they put up a sail made from seal gut, but the sail dried out very easily in the wind. Children were kept busy splashing the sail with containers of water.

On spring journeys the umiak was filled with the family's belongings and loaded on the sledge. When they came to open water, the family untied the boat and loaded the sledge and dogs onto the umiak for the water crossing. When they returned to their autumn camp, the umiak was piled high with meat, skins, and hides from the caribou hunt and loaded with all the goods the Eskimos had been collecting. They brought back soapstone for lamps and pots, roots and berries to make dyes, and shells to decorate their clothing.

How Eskimos Found Their Way

Eskimos were always studying the secrets of their environment and of the animals that lived in it. Their knowledge and understanding was handed down and expanded by generations of hunters. Eskimos noticed small changes in the color of ice, in patches of snow, and in the texture of water, and they studied the meanings of these tiny clues. But the signals given by the land could suddenly be obscured by fog, snow, rain, wind, glare, or darkness. Even short journeys could become perilous. Travel was a part of the Eskimo life. Men made regular excursions in search of food. Eskimos often traveled great distances — as much as two hundred miles. Small groups sometimes traveled together or an individual would go alone. They were skillful travelers.

When making a long journey to an unfamiliar area, the traveler would try to find someone who knew the country and could draw a map. Eskimos observed the landscape very carefully, took notice of all the details, and could draw very accurate maps on pieces of dried gut. They told directions from the sun, stars, or prevailing winds. Wind blew the snow into rows of snow mounds. They marked directions as they followed or crossed these rows. They measured distances by "sleepings," the number of times they stopped to sleep. Time could not easily be measured by the sun in the Arctic.

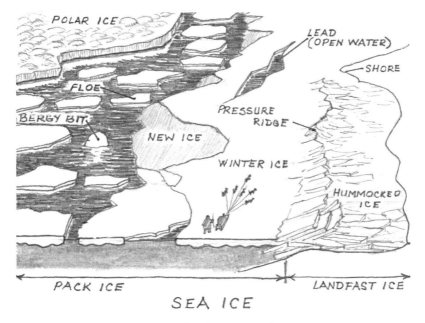

POLAR ICE

LEAD
(OPEN WATER)

SHORE

FLOE

PRESSURE
RIDGE

BERGY BIT

NEW ICE

WINTER ICE

HUMMOCKED
ICE

PACK ICE

LANDFAST ICE

SEA ICE

Sometimes they marked routes by setting stones on end at prominent points. Sledge routes that offered the best terrain for travel could sometimes be used as trails by other hunters — but travel conditions changed abruptly.

Eskimos seldom turned back once they set out on a journey, regardless of the difficulties they faced. But they were wise enough not to begin traveling if they thought there was danger involved. They refused to travel in any kind of weather in which they could easily lose their way.

Every hunter needed to understand the behavior of animals, but it was equally important to understand the behavior of ice. Eskimos studied every move and change in the ice. They judged the safety of ice by its color. Water shows through thin, clear ice making it appear very dark; as it thickens, it becomes gray. Hunters knew that even gray ice was not uniform. There were always patches of thin ice, and they needed to watch the ice carefully to guide their dog teams safely. Holes, cracks, and areas of weak ice were easily hidden by drifting snow.

Eskimos were always looking for signs of game whenever they traveled, but they still kept alert for unexpected situations, changes in their surroundings, or indications of changing weather conditions. Eskimos noticed that stars twinkled and danced noticeably a day or two before a storm wind. During calm, clear weather stars do not twinkle as much. Warmer weather often preceded a storm and temperatures often dropped near the end of a storm.

Every hunter's knowledge went beyond what was essential for ordinary travel and hunting. He also had a large store of information that he could call on in emergency situations. Eskimos learned the best way to walk on thin ice by observing polar bears. A man would spread his legs as wide as possible and slide his feet quickly along the ice. If he still could not make it to safe ice he would lie flat and squirm along with arms and legs stretched out. No Eskimos would ever give a demonstration of the technique on thin ice to show off his skill or even to teach someone else. Eskimos could not understand people doing dangerous things for excitement or competition. Eskimos never took unnecessary risks.

Eskimo hunters and travelers had to be creative and imaginative. They frequently needed these skills to make or repair equipment along their way. When they faced a problem, they devised a solution. Eskimos rarely gave up a task until it was completed, and they realized that jobs not done well caused more work in the long run. A hunter tried to use as little energy as possible and always looked for shortcuts. Energy was a valuable commodity. Eskimos often traveled a greater distance to follow the smoothest trail and avoid rough places. In the long run this used much less energy.

Other Kinds of Eskimo Houses

CHAPTER SIX

Tents

Eskimos changed the kinds of dwellings they lived in to meet different needs. The climate, the materials available, and the hunting activities they were pursuing influenced the kinds of houses needed at different times of the year. Even though their homes were temporary structures, they built neat and efficient houses.

Summer settlements were encampments of tents. When snowhouses were no longer comfortable or practical, most Eskimos moved into tents. The change was as pleasant as the change to the igloo in the cold and windy autumn weather. Camps of tents were set up at caribou crossings and at fishing sites.

Different groups made different kinds of tents. Some people pitched tents that were cone-shaped like tipis.

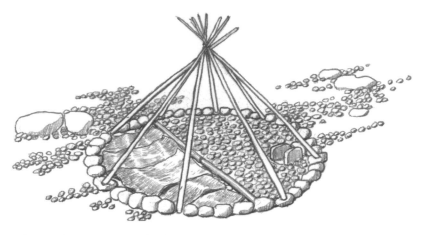

First they marked the floor size with a ring of large stones. Since wood for poles was scarce, these tents were sometimes constructed with only one pole. The pole rested on a flat stone in the center of the circle. Strong sealskin thongs were attached at the top of the pole and fastened to the heavy stones at the base of the tent. The sealskin cover was stretched over this frame, pulled tight at the bottom, and held in place under the ring of stones. Stones were often placed inside the tent leaning against the outer ring. This helped the tent withstand the strong Arctic winds. These tents were usually pitched by the men with some help from the women.

The woman set up the inside. She divided the tent into two sections by placing a line of flat stones across the floor. She covered the sleeping area at the back of the tent with furs. The kitchen and work area was at the front. Usually the fireplace was outside to keep smoke out of the house. She gathered heather for fuel.

Some people made a ridge-type tent. Sometimes there were crossed poles at the front and back of the tent with a pole or thong between them. Sometimes the tent was cone-shaped at the back with a ridge pole coming from the center of the cone to crossed poles in the front. The tent cover was either seal or caribou skin. The hair was left on the back part of the tent skins to keep the sleeping area somewhat dark during the constant daylight. The front part was of dehaired and

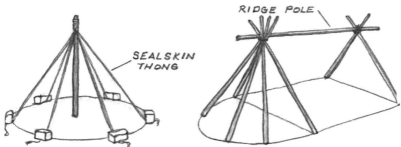

transparent skin, which let in light. Wooden poles were used for the frame. In some places, driftwood floated down from the forests, in others, people traveled or traded for their poles. The poles were as light as possible and the tents as small as possible to keep packs light when traveling.

Autumn Houses

There was often an unpleasant period between seasons when neither igloo nor tent was comfortable. Eskimos had several forms of dwellings that they used at these times. They called them *qarmat* or autumn houses since that was the season when they were usually needed. They were also used to some extent in the spring.

Sometimes Eskimos came upon ruins of houses that had been built long ago by different people, and they built *qarmat* on these sites. Men used the building materials scattered around to make a house, or they made temporary repairs to the ruins. Partial walls built of stone, earth, whale skulls, and bones were sometimes still standing. They repaired the damaged sections and filled in the cracks with moss. A tent cover or skin of some kind was used for the roof. They made a platform inside with flat stones. These sites were probably the remains of the winter homes of Thule people. Eskimos returned to these homes for as many autumns as they found this a favorable place.

Similar *qarmat* were built in areas where there had been no previous dwellings. They were oval or rectangular structures built of stone or sod to a height of five or six feet. Rafters of wood or large bones were placed across the walls, and two layers of sealskins with a layer of moss between them were placed over the rafters.

These houses often had a narrow passage excavated in the ground with the entrance below the floor. They had a platform at the back as in most Eskimo dwellings. Usually two families lived in the house. Each family had a place at the side for their stone lamp and for storage. Families returned to these houses making only minor repairs year after year.

Often an incomplete snowhouse was used as a transitional dwelling between seasons. Instead of the domed roof, a flat tent cover was spread over the walls. These half-igloo, half-tent structures were used either in autumn, before the snow was firm enough for blocks to be inclined, or in the spring, when the heat of the sun made the snowhouse unsafe. This was a dark and rather damp home, and families were glad when it could be abandoned for igloo or tent.

There were times in autumn when it was too cold to live in a tent but the snow was not deep enough to build an igloo. Some people built rectangular ice houses. The

walls were made of slabs of ice six or seven inches thick that were cut from river or lake ice using an ice chisel. The ice chisel was made of pointed hard bone fastened to a wooden shaft with skin thongs. Several men worked together cutting and hauling the blocks of ice and building the house. Each ice slab was about five by three feet in size, and eight to ten blocks were needed for a hut. The men made a hole in the corner of each block, tied a sealskin thong through it, and dragged the block to the building site. A mixture of snow and water was used as mortar to hold the blocks together. Tent skins were stretched over the walls for the roof and a doorway was cut at a joint between blocks of ice. Ice does not insulate as well as snow, but it made a satisfactory temporary house between seasons.

Sod and Wood Shelters

In Alaska and other Arctic regions where driftwood and large whale bones were available, Eskimos used these materials to contruct houses. These houses were usually built into a hillside and many of the same principles used in igloo building were applied. They used air-capture to heat their homes. The house was entered by a tunnel below the floor level. Dogs could find shelter from blizzards in the tunnel passageway. Since these houses required excavation and much labor, they were often built for more than one family. Each family had a

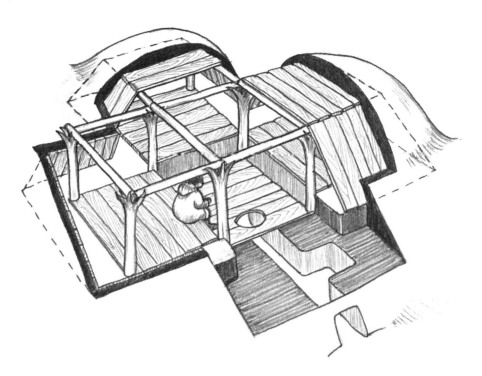

living area about seven feet square, and they usually
shared a common room about eight feet square. Tree
trunks were placed at the corner of each square with
the wide end upward and roots trimmed off. The corner posts were connected by small tree trunks around
the four sides of the squares, and the walls and roof
were built of split logs that leaned against the support-
ing logs. The house was covered with sod, with the grass
side against the wood frame. Then earth was shoveled
over the sod. The inside plan was very similar to an
igloo. There was usually a platform or bench across the
back of the house and a cooking lamp and drying rack
for each family.

Eskimos Today

The whalers, fur traders, missionaries, miners, and oil-men who came to the Arctic brought many changes to the Eskimos over the years. Most of the men who came did not appreciate the Eskimos' knowledge of the world around them. These newcomers gave little considera-tion to the land and less to the future. The animal pop-ulation that shared the Arctic with the Eskimos has been greatly reduced. The knives, rifles, matches, steel needles, flour, sugar, and factory-made goods brought to the Arctic gradually replaced Eskimo goods. Trap-ping fur-bearing animals became increasingly impor-tant as a way to trade for these new things. In more recent times, Eskimos have found themselves needing money and having to cope with jobs based on nine-to-five, temperate-zone hours that seem out of keeping with the rhythms of light and darkness in the polar north.

Eskimos no longer make everything they need with the tools they have made themselves. They now live in one place in clapboard bungalows. They purchase modern clothing from mail-order catalogs and they travel in snowmobiles, airplanes, and motorboats. These changes have caused serious problems in Eskimos' lives. They have substituted white man's food for Eskimo food and have suffered from nutritional deficiencies. Many families are drifting apart and have lost the feeling of interdependence that traditional Eskimo families had. Some people are idle and feel useless. The sharing concepts of Eskimo communities are being replaced by materialistic values of the modern world. Old ways and beliefs persist beside the newer ways, and many people feel confused by these conflicts. Widespread changes have taken place in a short time. There are Eskimo people who lived in igloos and tents who have watched men landing on the moon on their televisions. Old ways were hard, and in many ways their lives are better now. But a hard life can be very good and very happy.

Eskimos today face many problems and uncertainties, but they are trying to bring the good things from their traditional way of life with them as they meet these challenges. Because Eskimos live in such harsh and remote regions, the modern world has not intruded very much on their culture until recent times. They have been able to maintain their traditional way of life longer than many of the world's cultures, and they are confronting the modern world with more cultural unity. They have established organizations to represent their interests to the government and have made many positive steps in gaining control over their land and its resources. For many Eskimo communities in Canada, their art has become a major business. They have organized cooperatives that produce and sell Eskimo paintings, prints, sculpture, and craft products. Eskimo culture has always been very adaptive. Today Eskimos are adapting to the white man's world rather than to the Arctic, while striving to retain their harmony with the land.

Other Books of Interest to Children

Nonfiction

Alexander, Bryan, and Cherry Alexander. *An Eskimo Family.* Minneapolis: Lerner Publications Co., 1985.

Anderson, Madelyn Klein. *Greenland: Island at the Top of the World.* New York: Dodd, Mead & Co., 1983.

Cheney, Cora. *Alaska: Indians, Eskimos, Russians and the Rest.* New York: Dodd, Mead & Co., 1980.

Cleaver, Elizabeth. *The Enchanted Caribou.* New York: Atheneum, 1985.

"The Eskimos of Alaska." Cobblestone Magazine 6, no. 11 (November 1985).

Gillham, Charles E. *Medicine Men of Hooper Bay.* New York: Macmillan Co., 1955.

Gubok, Shirley. *The Art of the Eskimo.* New York: Harper & Row, 1964.

Hiscock, Bruce. *Tundra: The Arctic Land.* New York: Atheneum, 1986.

Lisker, Tom. *First to the Top of the World: Admiral Peary at the North Pole.* New York: Contemporary Perspectives, Inc., 1978.

Meyer, Carolyn. *Eskimos: Growing Up in a Changing Culture.* New York: Atheneum, 1977.

Pine, Tillie S. and Joseph Levine. *The Eskimos Knew.* New York: McGraw-Hill, 1962.

Purdy, Susan, and Cass R. Sandak. *Eskimos: A Civilization Project Book.* New York: Franklin Watts, 1982.

Rasmussen, Knud, ed. *Beyond the High Hills/A Book of Eskimo Poems.* Cleveland: World Publishing Co., 1961.

Williams, Terry Tempest, and Ted Major. *The Secret Language of Snow*. San Francisco: Sierra Club/Pantheon Books, 1984.

Fiction

Andrews, Jan. *Very Last First Time*. New York: Atheneum, 1986.

Codd, Carol. *Chooki and the Ptarmigan*. New York: Walker & Co., 1976.

Doone, Radko. *Nuvat the Brave*. Philadelphia: Macrae-Smith, 1934.

George, Jean Craighead. *Julie of the Wolves*. New York: Harper & Row, 1972.

————. *Water Sky*. New York: Harper & Row, 1987.

Houston, James. *Akavak*. New York: Harcourt, Brace & World, 1968.

————. *The White Archer*. New York: Harcourt, Brace & World, 1967.

————. *Wolf Run*. New York: Harcourt Brace Jovanovich, 1971.

Luenn, Nancy. *Arctic Unicorn*. New York: Atheneum, 1986.

O'Dell, Scott. *Black Star, Bright Dawn*. Boston: Houghton Mifflin Co., 1988.

Paulsen, Gary. *Dogsong*. New York: Bradbury Press, 1985.

Robinson, Tom D. *An Eskimo Birthday*. New York: Dodd, Mead & Co., 1975.

Rogers, Jean. *Goodbye, My Island*. New York: Greenwillow Books, 1983.

Sperry, Armstrong. *One Day with Tuktu an Eskimo Boy*. Chicago: John C. Winston Co., 1935.

Bibliography

Aigner, Jean S. "Early Arctic Settlements in North America." *Scientific American* 253, no. 5 (November 1985): 160–69.

Armstrong, Terrance, and Brian Roberts. "Illustrated Ice Glossary." *The Polar Record* 8, no. 52; 9, no. 59 (January 1956, May 1958): 4–12, 90–96.

Balikci, Asen. *The Netsilik Eskimo.* Garden City, N.Y.: Natural History Press, 1970.

Birket-Smith, Kaj. *The Caribou Eskimos.* Vol. 5 of the *Report of the Fifth Thule Expedition 1921–25.* Copenhagen: Gyldendalske Boghandel, Nordisk Forlag, 1929.

———. *Ethnographical Collections from the Northwest Passage.* Vol. 6, no. 2, of the *Report of the Fifth Thule Expedition 1921–24.* Copenhagen: Gyldendalske Boghandel, Nordisk Forlag, 1945.

Brown, G. Malcolm. "Cold Acclimatization in Eskimo." *Arctic* 7, nos. 2, 3 (December 1955): 343–51.

Carmichael, Hugh. "The Aurora." *The Polar Record* 4, no 25 (January 1943): 12–16.

Damas, David, ed. *Arctic.* Handbook of the North American Indians, edited by William C. Sturtevant, vol. 5. Washington, D.C.: Smithsonian Institution, 1984.

Debenham, Frank, ed. "Formation and Movement of Sea Ice." *The Polar Record* 4, no. 27 (January 1944): 128–133.

———. "Friction on Sledge Runners." *The Polar Record* 4, no. 25 (January 1943): 7–11.

———. "Igloos in the Alps." *The Polar Record* 3, no. 23 (January 1942): 512–16.

Dekin, Albert A., Jr. "Sealed in Time." *National Geographic* 171, no. 6 (June 1987): 824–36.

Eber, Dorothy. *Pitseolak: Pictures Out of My Life.* Seattle: University of Washington Press, 1971.

Fitch, James Marston, and Daniel P. Branch. "Primitive Architecture and Climate." *Scientific American* 203, no. 6 (December 1960): 134–44.

Flaherty, Robert. *Nanook of the North.* New York: Windmill Books, 1971.

Forde, C. Daryll. *Habitat, Economy and Society.* New York: E. P. Dutton & Co., 1934.

Freuchen, Dagmar, ed. *Peter Freuchen's Book of the Eskimos.* Cleveland: World Publishing Co., 1961.

Freuchen, Peter. *Eskimo.* New York: Grosset & Dunlap, 1931.

———. *Ivalu, the Eskimo Wife.* New York: Lee Furman, 1935. Reprint. New York: AMS Press, 1975.

Handy, Richard L. "The Igloo and the Natural Bridge as Ultimate Structures." *Arctic* 26, no. 4 (December 1973): 276–80.

Hanssen, Captain Helmer, Dr. S. Hadwen, and Andrew Croft. "Sledge Dogs." *The Polar Record*, no. 13 (January 1937): 57–81.

Jacobs, Martina Magenau, and James P. Richardson III, ed. *Arctic Life: Challenge to Survive*. Pittsburgh: Carnegie Institute, 1983.

Jenness, D. Vol. 12 of the *The Life of the Copper Eskimos. Report of the Canadian Arctic Expedition 1913–18*. Ottawa: F. A. Acland, 1922.

Johnston, Thomas F. "The Eskimo Songs of Northwestern Alaska." *Arctic* 29, no. 1 (March 1976): 7–18.

Kleinfeld, Judith. "Visual Memory in Village Eskimo and Urban Caucasian Children." *Arctic* 24, no. 2 (June 1971): 132–37.

Kopper, Philip. *The Smithsonian Book of North American Indians*. Washington, D.C.: Smithsonian Books, 1986.

Koppes, Wayne F. *A Report of Characteristics of Snow Houses and Their Practicability as a Form of Temporary Shelter*. Washington: National Research Council, 1948.

Lopez, Barry. *Arctic Dreams*. New York: Charles Scribner's Sons, 1986.

Manning, T. H. "Eskimo Stone Houses in Foxe Basin." *Arctic* 3, no. 2 (August 1950): 108–12.

————, and E. W. Manning, "The Preparation of Skins and Clothing in the Eastern Canadian Arctic." *The Polar Record* 4, no. 6 (July 1944): 156–69.

Marsh, D. B. "Life in a Snowhouse." *Natural History*, February 1951, 64–67.

————. "The Mudding of Sledge Runners." *The Polar Record* 4, no. 27 (January 1944): 139–41.

Mathiassen, Therkel. *Material Culture of the Iglulik Eskimos*. Vol. 6, no. 2, of the *Report of the Fifth Thule Expedition 1921–24*. Copenhagen: Gyldendalske Boghandel, Nordisk Forlag, 1928.

Nelson, Richard K. *Hunters of the Northern Ice*. Chicago: University of Chicago Press, 1969.

Peary, Robert E. *My Arctic Journal*. New York: Contemporary Publishing Co., 1893. Reprint. New York: AMS Press, 1975.

Polar Regions Atlas. Washington, D.C.: Central Intelligence Agency, 1978.

Porsild, A. E. "Edible Plants of the Arctic." *Arctic* 6, no. 1 (March 1953): 15–34.

Rapoport, Amos. *House Form and Culture*. Englewood Cliffs, N.J.: Prentice-Hall, Inc., 1969.

Rodahl, Kaare. "Hypervitaminosis." *Skrifter* 95, 1950.

————. "The Toxic Effect of Polar Bear Liver." *Skrifter* 92, 1949.

————. "Vitamin Sources in Arctic Regions." *Skrifter* 91, 1949.

Sater, John E., A. G. Ronhovde, and L. C. Van Allen. *Arctic Environment and Resources*. Washington, D.C.: Arctic Institute of North America, 1971.

Schaefer, Otto. "Eskimo Personality and Society Yesterday and Today." *Arctic* 26, no. 2 (June 1975): 87–91.

Stefansson, Vilhjalmur. "Clothes Make the Eskimo." *Natural History*, January 1955, 32–41, 51.

———. *Stefansson-Anderson Arctic Expedition.* Vol. 14, Anthropological Papers. American Museum of Natural History, New York, 1919. Reprint. New York: AMS Press, 1978.

Steltzer, Ulli. *Inuit.* Seattle: University of Washington Press, 1982.

Weeks, Wilford F., and Owen S. Lee. "Observations on the Physical Properties of Sea-Ice at Hopedale, Labrador." *Arctic* 11, no 3 (1958): 135–55.

Weyer, Edward Moffat. *The Eskimos.* New Haven, Conn.: Yale University Press, 1969. Reprint. Archon Books, 1969.

———. "Walrus Hunt." *Natural History,* January 1956, 28–32.

Whittaker, C. E. *Arctic Eskimo.* London: Seeley, Service & Co., 1937. Reprint. New York: AMS Press, 1976.

Zimmerly, David W. *Hooper Bay Kayak Construction.* Ottawa: National Museums of Canada, 1979.

Index